NORTH AMERICAN ANIMALS

Gray Squirrels

by Christina Leaf

BLASTOFF!
3
READERS

BELLWETHER MEDIA • MINNEAPOLIS, MN

Note to Librarians, Teachers, and Parents:

Blastoff! Readers are carefully developed by literacy experts and combine standards-based content with developmentally appropriate text.

Level 1 provides the most support through repetition of high-frequency words, light text, predictable sentence patterns, and strong visual support.

Level 2 offers early readers a bit more challenge through varied simple sentences, increased text load, and less repetition of high-frequency words.

Level 3 advances early-fluent readers toward fluency through increased text and concept load, less reliance on visuals, longer sentences, and more literary language.

Level 4 builds reading stamina by providing more text per page, increased use of punctuation, greater variation in sentence patterns, and increasingly challenging vocabulary.

Level 5 encourages children to move from "learning to read" to "reading to learn" by providing even more text, varied writing styles, and less familiar topics.

Whichever book is right for your reader, Blastoff! Readers are the perfect books to build confidence and encourage a love of reading that will last a lifetime!

This edition first published in 2015 by Bellwether Media, Inc.

No part of this publication may be reproduced in whole or in part without written permission of the publisher. For information regarding permission, write to Bellwether Media, Inc., Attention: Permissions Department, 5357 Penn Avenue South, Minneapolis, MN 55419.

Library of Congress Cataloging-in-Publication Data

Leaf, Christina.
  Gray Squirrels / by Christina Leaf.
    pages cm. – (Blastoff! Readers. North American Animals)
  Includes bibliographical references and index.
  Summary: "Simple text and full-color photography introduce beginning readers to gray squirrels. Developed by literacy experts for students in kindergarten through third grade"– Provided by publisher.
  Audience: Ages 5-8.
  Audience: K to Grade 3.
  ISBN 978-1-62617-187-9 (hardcover : alk. paper)
  1. Gray squirrel–Juvenile literature. I. Title.
  QL737.R68L43 2015
  599.36'2–dc23
                                                    2014040721

Printed in the United States of America, North Mankato, MN.

Table of Contents

What Are Gray Squirrels?

Gray squirrels are common **rodents** in North America.

In the Wild

N
W E
S

Extinct

Extinct in the Wild

Critically Endangered

Endangered

Vulnerable

Near Threatened

Least Concern

gray squirrel range = ▢

conservation status: least concern

These **mammals** live in forests and backyards in the eastern United States and into Canada. Small numbers are found along the Pacific coast.

Identify a Gray Squirrel

fluffy tail   **pointy ears**   **four front teeth**

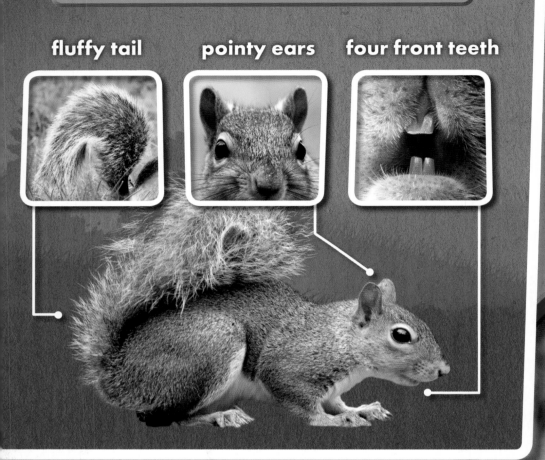

The squirrels are named
for their gray color.

However, some may have reddish or brown fur. Others can be all black or all white.

Gray squirrels are only 18 to 20 inches (46 to 51 centimeters) long. A fluffy tail makes up half of this length.

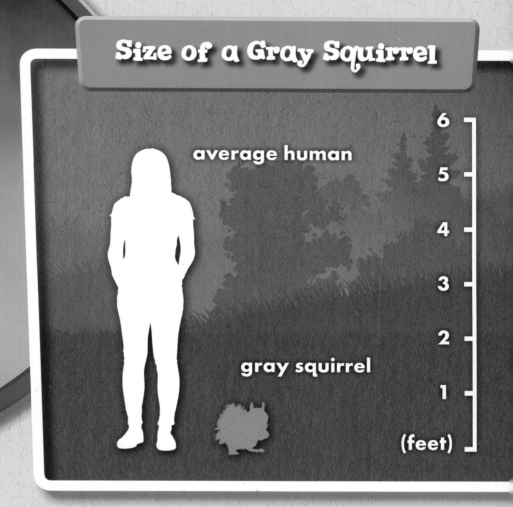

Size of a Gray Squirrel

average human

gray squirrel

6
5
4
3
2
1
(feet)

Their long tails help them balance on branches. They also provide warmth in winter and shade in summer.

Climbing Trees

Gray squirrels make their nests in tree holes. They also build **dreys** high in treetops.

The animals **scamper** up trees
to their nests. Sharp nails give
them good **grip**. They climb
headfirst on the way down.

Animals to Avoid

rat snakes

red foxes

bobcats

raccoons

red-tailed hawks

great horned owls

A gray squirrel makes clicking sounds when it sees danger. This warns other squirrels in the area to run.

They dash through treetops to escape hawks, foxes, and other **predators**.

Gray squirrels are **omnivores**. Acorns and other nuts are favorite foods. Strong teeth help the squirrels crack the shells.

beechnuts

acorns

butternuts

black cherries

cherry blossoms

hickory nuts

Other foods include berries, flowers, insects, and bird eggs. Squirrels that live near people often steal seeds from bird feeders.

15

Gray squirrels store food in late summer and early fall. They bury nuts all over their **territory**.

In winter, the squirrels return to their hiding spots. Their sharp noses sniff out the buried nuts.

A female gray squirrel usually has two litters in a year. **Kittens** are born in late winter and summer. Mom teaches them what to eat and how to run through treetops.

Baby Facts

Names for babies:	kittens, kits, pups
Size of litter:	2 to 4 kittens
Length of pregnancy:	44 days
Time spent with parents:	8 to 14 weeks (winter) 20 weeks (summer)

Winter babies leave the nest in early summer. The second litter may stay with mom through December.

Then it is time to build their own nests!

Glossary

dreys—squirrel nests in treetops; dreys are made of twigs and leaves.

grip—a tight hold

kittens—baby squirrels

mammals—warm-blooded animals that have backbones and feed their young milk

omnivores—animals that eat both plants and animals

predators—animals that hunt other animals for food

rodents—small animals that gnaw on their food

scamper—to run quickly

territory—the land area where an animal lives

To Learn More

AT THE LIBRARY

Lundgren, Julie K. *Squirrels*. Vero Beach, Fla.: Rourke Pub., 2011.

Peet, Bill. *Merle the High Flying Squirrel*. Boston, Mass.: Houghton Mifflin, 1974.

Thomas, Isabel. *Squirrel*. Chicago, Ill.: Capstone Heinemann Library, 2014.

ON THE WEB

Learning more about gray squirrels is as easy as 1, 2, 3.

1. Go to www.factsurfer.com.

2. Enter "gray squirrels" into the search box.

3. Click the "Surf" button and you will see a list of related web sites.

With factsurfer.com, finding more information is just a click away.

Index

The images in this book are reproduced through the courtesy of: John L. Richbourg, front cover, p. 6 (bottom); Giedriius, pp. 4-5; arnaldo.jr, p. 6 (top left); Ed Phillips, p. 6 (top middle); N A Callow/ Newscom, p. 6 (top right); Paul Reeves Photography, pp. 6-7; MAC1, pp. 8-9; Doug Wechsler/ Animals Animals, p. 10; Erni, pp. 11, 21; Eric Isselee, p. 12 (top left, top right, & middle right); Svetlana Foote, p. 12 (middle left); Le Do, p. 12 (bottom left); mlorenz, p. 12 (bottom right); Brian Bevan/ Ardea/ Biosphoto, p. 13; Real_World_Stu, pp. 14-15; Petr Baumann, p. 15 (top left); Dionisvera, p. 15 (top right); Lars Kock, p. 15 (middle left); schab, p. 15 (middle right); AVprophoto, p. 15 (bottom left); JIANG HONGYAN, p. 15 (bottom right); Andrea Izzotti, p. 16; Paul Roedding, p. 17; PCHY, pp. 18-19; Becky Sheridan, p. 19; SallyNewcomb, p. 20.